BIBLE QUIZZES AND PUZZLES

by
Helen Pettigrew

BAKER BOOK HOUSE
Grand Rapids, Michigan

Copyright © 1971 by
Baker Book House Company

ISBN: 0-8010-6902-5

The following publishers have granted permission to reprint puzzles which originally appeared in their publications:
United Church of Canada Publishing House: 1, 16, 18, 49, 50, 51, 52, 53, 54, 55, 56, 57, 58
Sunday School Board, Southern Baptist Convention: 8, 9
David C. Cook Company: 2, 31, 32, 33, 34, 35, 43
Harvest Publications: 3, 27, 28, 29, 30
American Sunday School Union: 5, 6
Union Gospel Press: 7
Progressive Farmer: 46, 47, 48
Contact, Huntington, Ind.: 11, 22, 23
Scripture Press: 12, 13, 15, 17
Augsburg Publishing Company: 59, 60
Standard Publishing: 36, 37, 38, 39, 40, 41
Seventh-day Adventist Publishing Company: 42, 44, 45
Christian, London, England: 4, 21
Sunday Companion, London, England: 14, 24, 25
Home Words, London, England: 10, 19, 20, 26

Printed in the United States of America

BIBLE QUIZZES AND PUZZLES

CONTENTS

1. Mothers in the Bible 5
2. Imaginary Greeting to Mother 6
3. Double Match in Relationships 7
4. The Elder Brother (or Sister) 8
5. Brothers in the Square 9
6. Making Names of Names 10
7. Featuring Four-letter Names in the Bible 11
8. Much in a Name 12
9. Relatives 13
10. Fathers and Mothers 14
11. Also — One of Three 15
12. Hidden Names 16
13. "Thank You" Notes 17
14. Descriptive Words 18
15. Songs from the Bible 19
16. "What Time I Am Afraid" 20
17. Biblical Proportions 21
18. Paul 22
19. A Question of Concern 23
20. Early Churches 24
21. Hidden Couplet About Paul 25
22. They Would Not 26
23. The Gracious Ones 27
24. If 28
25. Bible Crossword Puzzle in Numbers 29
26. Read Down and Find 30
27. Crowded Line 31
28. "And of the Prophets" . . . and Others 32
29. They Changed 33
30. Heavenly Space 34

31.	"The Unknown God"	35
32.	Both Rhyme and Reason	36
33.	Read the Square Clockwise	37
34.	Choice Within a Choice	38
35.	"Frustrations" in the Bible	39
36.	Archaeological Discoveries	40
37.	"Now the Day Is Over"	41
38.	Word Acrostic	42
39.	Square of Squares	43
40.	On the Way	44
41.	Find the Proverb	45
42.	Featuring Food	46
43.	Bird, Beast, and Insect	47
44.	Triple Proportion	48
45.	Acrostic	49
46.	How Many?	50
47.	The Parables	51
48.	Who?	52
49.	"Dare to Be a Daniel"	53
50.	Quote — Misquote	54
51.	Sally's Complaint	55
52.	"Judge" for Yourself	56
53.	The Nameless Ones	57
54.	"Name" the Italics	58
55.	Down the Alphabet	59
56.	This is _ _ _ _ _ Speaking	60
57.	They Were "Human"	61
58.	What Were They Doing?	62
59.	Questions in the Bible (Part 1)	63
60.	Questions in the Bible (Part 2)	64
Answers		65

1. Mothers in the Bible

1. This mother of Reuben was Jacob's first wife
2. She bore Isaac late in her life
3. She encouraged her son's gracious widow to wed
4. She took her young boy, to the wilderness fled
5. She hid Joshua's spies, a very brave thing
6. From her sprang the line of the prophesied King
7. Bringing Samuel to Eli, she fulfilled her word
8. She said, I've received a man from the Lord
9. She gave birth to one known as the wisest of men
10. Her two boys Jacob loved more than his other ten
11. Saluted by Mary, great was her joy
12. She was good to Elisha and he raised her dead boy
13. She looked at the cross, and she went to the tomb
14. She looked out a window and was thrown from her room
15. She slew her grandchildren so she could be queen
16. As a judge was this "Mother in Israel" seen
17. She helped one son get what belonged to another
18. She was Timothy's good and commendable mother

(a) Eve
(b) Jezebel
(c) The woman of Shunem
(d) Bathsheba
(e) Elizabeth
(f) Salome
(g) Deborah
(h) Athaliah
(i) Rahab
(j) Naomi
(k) Eunice
(l) Leah
(m) Sarah
(n) Hagar
(o) Rebekah
(p) Rachel
(q) Ruth
(r) Hannah

2. Imaginary Greeting to Mother

Below are couplets which — by a stretch of the imagination — could have been written by boys or young men in the Bible to their mothers. At the right are the names of the supposed writers and the mothers to whom the couplets were addressed. One is a grandmother. And one mother was not living when the couplet would have been written.

1. Only through your help, d e a r Mother,
   I stole the birthright from my brother.
2. To the wilderness we fled
   And there you wept for me as dead.
3. True, 'twas an Egyptian found me,
   But, your arms were soon around me.
4. In the temple you "installed" me
   There the Lord's voice clearly called me.
5. More than all the other ten
   Dad loved your children, me and Ben.
6. Mother dear, Grandmother, too,
   The apostle Paul spoke well of you.
7. Was your faith strong as that of Dad
   When he built an altar for his lad?
8. Grandmother, I was saved from you.
   Oh, what a cruel thing to do!
9. In place of your slain son I came.
   You thought of this, and hence my name.
10. You made a good choice, Mother dear —
    It wasn't Moab, it was here.

(a) Ishmael to Hagar
(b) Moses to Jochebed
(c) Obed to Ruth
(d) Timothy to Eunice
(e) Joash to Athaliah
(f) Isaac to Sarah
(g) Jacob to Rebekah
(h) Joseph to Rachel
(i) Samuel to Hannah
(j) Seth to Eve

3. Double Match in Relationships

Each correct match is worth 5 points, and each correct double match is worth 10 points. With a score of 90 or more you are a. evidently familiar with relationships in the Bible and A. maker of an excellent score.

1. Saul was the	a. son-in-law of Jethro and	A. great-grandfather of Manasseh
2. Joseph was the	b. sister of Laban and	B. grandmother of Timothy
3. Moses was the	c. husband of Rebekah and	C. Daughter-in-law of Terah
4. Isaac was the	d. mother of Boaz and	D. son of Jochebed
5. Sarah was the	e. son of Zebedee and	E. father of Enos
6. Rebekah was the	f. son of Kish and	F. father of Ephraim
7. Lois was the	g. son of Adam and	G. grandmother of Joseph
8. James was the	h. brother of Benjamin and	H. brother of John
9. Rahab was the	i. mother of Eunice and	I. father of Jonathan
10. Seth was the	j. mother of Isaac and	J. grandmother of Obed

4. The Elder Brother (or Sister)

The elder brother in the parable of The Prodigal Son showed an envious spirit. Below are instances of elder brothers and sisters, and in some cases their attitude toward the younger. Each number is worth 10 points. A score of 90 plus is excellent, 75-90 good, and 60-70 fair. In one instance the "elder brother" is a twin.

1. He acted as spokesman for his younger brother who felt he was not a good enough speaker to do the work God told him to do.
2. He was cheated by his younger brother and threatened vengeance.
3. He was killed by Herod. His younger brother wrote the last book of the Bible.
4. He (the eldest of all) was angry with his youngest brother for showing an interest in the challenge of Goliath.
5. He was separated from his younger brother for years, and was reunited during a famine.
6. This elder sister was given preference by their father when a young man asked for the younger one to be his wife.
7. The elder brother received a lesser blessing than the younger, from their grandfather.
8. His sacrifice was not acceptable to God, as was his younger brother's.
9. The elder brother as well as the younger failed to live up to their father's reputation, as judges.
10. When their brother died, the elder sister said to the younger, "The Master is come, and calleth for thee."

5. Brothers in the Square

Names of brothers in the Bible fill the square below. Beginning with the respective numbers, can you spell them all, moving one letter at a time, to the right, left, up or down? There will be no catercornered lines and all squares will have been reached. You will need a pencil, probably one with an eraser. Begin with E in the upper left, and end with S one square over from upper right.

¹E	S	N	³A	N	D	S	E
U	A	A	⁴B	E	R	A	M
²L	A	B	E	W	M	¹¹J	I
⁵L	A	J	N	A	I	H	N
A	M	I	N	R	⁸J	P	O
Z	⁶M	O	P	H	A	L	¹⁰H
A	S	S	⁷E	H	P	E	B
R	U	E	S	E	T	H	⁹A

1. Jacob's brother
2. Rebekah's brother
3. Peter's brother
4. Joseph's brother
5. Brother of Mary and Martha
6. Aaron's brother
7. Manasseh's brother
8. Brother of Shem and Ham
9. Cain's brother
10. Phinehas' brother
11. John the Disciple's brother

6. Making Names of Names

Suffix AB to a patient man, JOB, and have a son of Joktan, JOBAB. Prefix R to the husband of Jezebel, AHAB, and have the mother of Boaz, RAHAB. In the same way, can you identify the names in each number?

1. Prefix JO to a prophet, and have a friend of David.
2. Suffix IEL to a son of Jacob, and have a brave young man, also a book of the Old Testament.
3. Prefix SUS to a prophetess, and have a woman who ministered to Jesus.
4. Prefix SAM to a son of Beni, and have the last of the judges, also a book of the Old Testament.
5. Suffix IAS to a tetrarch and have his sister-in-law.
6. Prefix JO to a Canaanitess, and have the successor of Moses, also a book of the Old Testament.
7. Suffix AH to the father of Balak, and have the wife of Moses.
8. Prefix BATH to a son of Bichri, and have the mother of Solomon.
9. Suffix AN to a son of Noah, and have an enemy of the Jews.
10. Suffix JAH to a high priest, and have a prophet.

7. Featuring Four-letter Names in the Bible

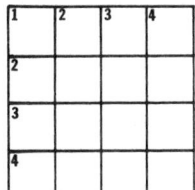

1. Gospel writer
2. Shakespeare's river
3. The _____ of Sharon
4. Had knowledge (Gen. 28:16)

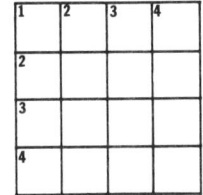

1. First man
2. U.S. coin
3. Word used after a prayer
4. Repair (Matt. 4:21)

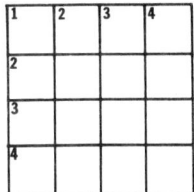

1. Prophet, book of the Old Testament
2. _____ me as one of thy hired servants (Luke 15:19)
3. Vegetable
4. Line of stitching (John 19:23)

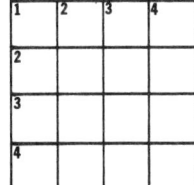

1. Sister of Rachel (Gen. 29:16)
2. A scribe, book of the Old Testament
3. Child of Shem (Gen. 10:22)
4. Part of a harness

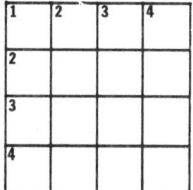

1. Disciple, Gospel writer
2. Butter substitute
3. City (II Kings 18:34)
4. He built the ark

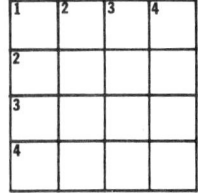

1. Grandmother of Timothy (II Tim. 1:5)
2. Turn out
3. Small island
4. Walk (Job 31:7)

8. Much in a Name

Names meant much in Bible times. "Thou shalt call his name JESUS," Joseph was told in a dream, "for he shall save his people from their sins" (Matt. 1:21). Eve called her firstborn son Cain, and said, "I have gotten a man from the Lord (Gen. 4:1). Below are 10 instances of sons being named for special reasons. Each name filled in correctly is worth 10 points. With a score of 90 you may call yourself, Aneas, meaning praiseworthy, *or Esther, meaning* star.

1. Eve called her son _____, saying he was given in place of another who was slain.

2. A princess adopted a child and named him _____, because he was drawn out of the water.

3. Leah said, "A troop cometh," and she called the child _____.

4. Hannah called her son _____ saying, "Because I have asked him of the Lord."

5. Joseph called his son _____, "For God hath caused me to be fruitful in the land of my affliction."

6. Moses called his son _____, for he said; "I have been a stranger in a strange land."

7. Rachel named her son _____ and said, "The Lord shall add to me another son."

8. David called his son _____ which means "peaceful." The son had a long, peaceful reign.

9. Elizabeth named her son _____, though there was no one with that name in the family.

10. Isaac's son was named _____, which means "hairy."

9. Relatives

Sarah's husband was Isaac's _____, _____. *The blanks should be filled in with* father, *and* Abraham. *There are two blanks in each line below. The first blank is worth 6 points, the second 4. A score of 80 is good, 90 better, and 100 best. If you score below 60, you may have been a bit blank yourself in answering this quiz.*

1. Benjamin's mother was Joseph's _____, _____.
2. Joseph's father was Ephraim's _____, _____.
3. Mary's sister was Lazarus' _____, _____.
4. Lois's grandson was Eunice's _____, _____.
5. Moses' mother was Miriam's _____, _____.
6. James' father was John's _____, _____.
7. Boaz' wife was Obed's _____, _____.
8. Samuel's mother was Elkanah's _____, _____.
9. Abraham's nephew was Terah's _____, _____.
10. Jacob's mother was Laban's _____, _____.

10. Fathers and Mothers

Can you sort them out? Put a letter against each figure.

1. Whose mother is mentioned in praise by Paul? (a) Rehoboam's
2. Whose father was Israel's first king, Saul? (b) Obed's
3. Whose mother would have the royal seed slain? (c) Joseph's
4. Whose father stored Egypt's fields of grain? (d) Samuel's
5. Whose father saw a great plague of flies? (e) Isaac's
6. Whose mother sheltered a couple of spies? (f) Solomon's
7. Whose mother gleaned in the fields of corn? (g) Timothy's
8. Whose father over in Ur was born? (h) Ahaziah's
9. Whose father stole from his twin brother? (i) Gershom's
10. Whose mother was loved when the wife of another? (j) Ephraim's
11. Whose mother brought him to Eli, the priest? (k) Boaz'
12. Whose father said a good man is good to his beast? (l) Jonathan's

11. Also — One of Three

1. David reigned forty years. So did: (a) Solomon (b) Saul (c) Jehu
2. Paul was a tentmaker. So was: (a) Hannah (b) Priscilla (c) Sapphira
3. Absalom was handsome. So was: (a) Mordecai (b) Joseph (c) Esau
4. Jude has only one chapter. So has: (a) II Timothy (b) Ezra (c) Philemon
5. Matthew was a tax collector. So was: (a) Zacchaeus (b) Thomas (c) Nicodemus
6. Jacob had a vision. So had: (a) Demetrius (b) Lazarus (c) Peter
7. Isaac had two sons. So had: (a) Noah (b) Boaz (c) Eli
8. A song is sung by Deborah and Barak. A song is also sung by: (a) Abraham (b) Samson (c) Moses
9. Paul was taken for a god. So was: (a) Apollos (b) Silas (c) Barnabas
10. Naomi was Ruth's mother-in-law. So later was: (a) Lois (b) Rahab (c) Dorcas
11. We associate John the Baptist with the wilderness. Also: (a) Shem (b) Cain (c) Ishmael
12. Jacob's grandson Ephraim was made head of a tribe. So was another grandson: (a) Levi (b) Manasseh (c) Cush

12. Hidden Names

In each of the numbers below there is a name of some Bible character hidden, and there is a hint in the line as to who the character might be.

1. He seemed avid to slay the big Philistine.
2. Do be diligent and loyal as your mother was to Naomi.
3. He came quickly and drew his net to the shore.
4. Yes, I last saw him with the apostle.
5. Was it in the lea he saw Laban's daughter?
6. Hello, is your grandmother in, Timothy?
7. At her request her husband the king spared her people.
8. Truly, Diana of the Ephesians would not charm this convert of Paul's.
9. Agrippa, ultimately it seems, would have wished to release him.
10. Will you have sauce with the pottage?
11. You might be strong enough to carry the flotsam and jetsam, son.
12. He could have little comfort in his sons as priests.

13. "Thank You" Notes

Imagine the "Thank You" verses below were sent by people in the Bible to some relative, or in one instance, friend. If Isaac had supposedly sent one to Rebekah (which he didn't) the answer would read, "To my wife Rebekah, from Isaac."

1. I thank you sincerely
   In this bit of verse
   For your practical wisdom
   In securing my burse.

   To my _____
   From _____

2. My husband is wealthy
   Kindhearted and clever
   For your help in this union
   My gratitude ever.

   To my _____
   From _____

3. This is to thank you
   For setting me straight
   When some Jews bent to kill me
   Were lying in wait.

   To my _____
   From _____

4. For saving my life
   This "Thank You" I send
   Though your father would slay me
   You're true to the end.

   To my _____
   From _____

5. Mine is well-watered land
   Under Jordan's blue sky.
   You gave me my choice
   And grateful am I.

   To my _____
   From _____

6. You've been truly good to me
   All the years through
   And now I'm a queen
   Thanks mainly to you.

   To my _____
   From _____

14. Descriptive Words

Each number below has two or more adjectives, or substantives, to be filled in. Most of them should be familiar. A score of 12 and over is "well and good," 9-12 is "fair and passing," and below 8 poor and disappointing.

1. How _____ upon the mountains are the feet of him that bringeth _____ tidings.
2. A _____ and a _____ heart, O God, thou wilt not despise.
3. A _____ son maketh a _____ father: but a _____ man despiseth his mother.
4. Saul and Jonathan were _____ and _____ in their lives, and in their death they were not divided.
5. . . . or ever the _____ cord be loosed, or the _____ bowl be broken . . .
6. If we confess our sins, he is _____ and _____ to forgive our sins . . .
7. And be ye _____ one to another, _____, forgiving one another . . .
8. . . . be ye therefore _____ as serpents, and _____ as doves.
9. Doth a fountain send forth at the same place _____ water and _____?
10. For my yoke is _____, and my burden is _____.
11. The law of the Lord is _____, converting the soul: the testimony of the Lord is _____, making _____ the simple.
12. . . . they are a _____ and _____ generation.
13. He maketh me to lie down in _____ pastures: he leadeth me beside the _____ waters.
14. A _____ answer turneth away wrath, but _____ words stir up anger.
15. I returned, and saw . . . that the race is not to the _____, nor the battle to the _____.

15. Songs from the Bible

"Abide with me," "My rest a stone," "I know that my Redeemer liveth," and many other excerpts from songs are based on the Bible. Below are other instances, and at the right are the authors, or people we connect with the excerpts. How many can you match?

1. And leap, ye lame, for joy
2. I will pass, I will pass, over you
3. Here am I, send me
4. Faith is the victory
5. Angels descending
6. They called to the rocks and the mountains
7. Almost persuaded
8. Here I raise my Ebenezer
9. A ruler once came to Jesus by night
10. He hideth my soul in the cleft of the rock
11. He is able to deliver thee
12. When He cometh to make up His jewels

(a) Moses
(b) John (in a vision)
(c) Nicodemus
(d) Daniel
(e) Peter
(f) Samuel
(g) Malachi
(h) Jacob
(i) The Children of Israel
(j) John (in a letter)
(k) Isaiah
(l) Agrippa

16. "What Time I Am Afraid"

Fear is a human and natural feeling under certain conditions. The cowardice lies in giving way to it. Below are instances of people in the Bible who experienced fear, though a majority demonstrated great courage at the time or later. Two or three are designated by their occupations or relationship in the answer.

1. This prophet was afraid of a wicked queen, and fled from her presence.
2. He was cupbearer to a king, but he was afraid when asked by the king to reveal the cause of his sadness.
3. A king seemed determined to slay this youth, but the king's son helped him escape.
4. He slew a man who was mistreating a fellow countryman. When he found there was a witness to his act, he fled.
5. He cheated his brother, and fled to escape revenge.
6. They were afraid and distressed upon finding a cup that had been planted in one of their sacks.
7. She realized she might be taking her life in her hands when she made a request of her husband, the king.
8. This king "prayed and cried to heaven" and his people were saved from a great army by the "angel of death."
9. He trembled when the men he was supposed to guard had a chance to escape.
10. He dwelt with his daughters in a cave, for he was afraid to live in Zoar.
11. He was afraid to own his allegiance to a man who had been betrayed.
12. All but two were fearful of entering the Promised Land because of the people they would have to overcome.

17. Biblical Proportions

Saul was the son of Kish and David was the son of Jesse. So we might say, Saul is to Kish as David is to Jesse. Or, as you are to complete the proportions below, Saul is to Kish as David is to X. How many proportions can you complete by substituting the name or word for X?

1. Sarah : Abraham :: Ruth : X
2. Samson : strong :: Moses: X
3. Pharaoh's dream : Joseph :: Belshazzar's dream : X
4. *Israel* : "Contender with God" :: *Peter* : X
5. Commandments : 10 :: Tribes of Israel : X
6. Luke : physician :: Lydia : X
8. Jordan : river :: Galilee: X
9. Elah : valley :: Pisgah : X
10. Cither : guitar :: psaltery : X
11. Last king of Israel : Hoshea :: last king of Judah : X
12. Psalms : David :: Proverbs : X
13. "Gospels" : Matthew, Mark, Luke and John :: "Pentateuch" : X
14. Cain : Abel :: Esau : X
15. Solomon : Bathsheba :: Benjamin : X
16. Pharaoh : Egypt :: Nebuchadnezzar : X
17. Ruth : Moabitess :: Elijah : X
18. Job : patience (or steadfastness) :: Solomon : X

18. Paul

1. Paul was (a) a Jew (b) part Jew and part Greek (c) Greek
2. He was born in Tarsus, noted for (a) its architecture (b) its Greek literature (c) its system of courts
3. His name was originally that of the (a) first king of Israel (b) last of the judges (c) prophet who followed Elijah
4. He was present at the death of (a) The Father of the Faithful (b) The Beloved Disciple (c) The first Christian martyr
5. He was as far as we know (a) often with Jesus (b) present only at the Sermon on the Mount (c) in contact with him only after the Resurrection
6. After his conversion, Paul straightway (a) retired to meditate and study (b) went back to Tarsus (c) preached Christ in the synagogue
7. He then (a) preached continuously for six years (b) spent some time in Arabia (c) went to Rome
8. He was one of the first two missionaries. The other was (a) Barnabas (b) Timothy (c) Silas
9. They were sent from the church at (a) Ephesus (b) Antioch (c) Jerusalem
10. On his first missionary journey Paul (a) cured a cripple at Lystra (b) had a vision at Phrygia (c) captured a runaway slave at Rome
11. As a result the people (a) put him in prison (b) thought they were gods (c) sent them away
12. On his second missionary journey Paul had with him (a) Barnabas and Mark (b) Mark (c) Timothy and Silas
13. At Troas he had a vision of (a) an angel warning him of danger (b) a great church at Jerusalem (c) a man of Macedonia calling for help
14. On this journey Paul and Silas were cast into prison. They (a) cried with a loud voice (b) escaped (c) prayed and sang praises to God

19. A Question of Concern

When you have filled in the blanks, arrange the letters according to their numbers in the blanks below and you will have a question from the Old Testament asked about a young man. The first letters of the words filled in will, reading down, tell the relationship of the young man to the questioner.

_ _ _ _ 4 12 20 2	Whose brothers were Shem and Japheth?
_ _ 1 23	Provided that (John 14:15)
_ _ _ _ _ _ 16 22 11 8 24 18	Last of the judges
_ _ _ _ 21 17 13 10	Paul and Silas prayed and ———— in prison (Acts 16:25)
_ _ _ _ 7 14 3 6	Full of wild oats (rare)
_ _ _ _ 9 5 15 19	Mount from which Moses viewed the Promised Land

_ _   _ _ _   _ _ _ _ _   _ _ _
1 2   3 4 5   6 7 8 9 10   11 12 13

_ _ _ _ _ _ _   _ _ _ _?
14 15 16 17 18 19 20   21 22 23 24

20. Early Churches

Beginning with any letter, and moving one letter at a time to the right, left, up, down, or across, can you spell the names of as many as five cities where early churches were established in the Bible?

A	T	N	A
R	L	I	P
I	O	H	P
N	C	M	E
H	T	U	S

21. Hidden Couplet About Paul

When you have filled in the blanks, can you find, reading down, a couplet about Paul? There will be one word to a line, and the words, with one exception, will be found in other words. One is complete.

_ _ _ _ _ _ _ _ Having number and variety (Eph. 3:10)

_ _ _ _ _ _ _ _ Asked authoritatively (Matt. 2:4)

_ _ _ _ _ _ _ _ Spent amiss — as Paul's life was not

_ _ _ _ _ _ _ _ Pastor (Eph. 3:7)

_ _ _ _ _ _ _ _ Paul was one more than once (Matt. 27:16)

_ _ _ _ _ _ _ _ One was cast off as disqualified — which Paul did not want to be (I Cor. 9:27)

_ _ _ _ _ _ _ _ Paul was not disobedient unto the _____ vision (Acts 26:19)

_ _ _ _ _ _ _ _ Bathed again

_ _ _ _ _ _ _ _ Steadfast, as Paul was (Luke 12:42)

_ _ _ _ _ _ _ _ Pertaining to (I Cor. 8:1)

_ _ _ _ _ _ _ _ Peter and Andrew were _____

_ _ _ _ _ _ _ _ Blight (Amos 4:9)

22. They Would Not

Some refusals in the Bible were good; others were not so good. Can you match the instances below with the people who "would not"?

1. He refused to sell his vineyard to a king.
2. He refused a "furlough" to visit home.
3. He refused to leave Elijah.
4. He refused to eat and drink the king's meat and wine.
5. He refused to bow down to Haman and do him reverence.
6. He refused to give his younger daughter in marriage before the elder.
7. He refused repeatedly to give a nation its freedom.
8. He refused to let an angel go without a blessing for himself.
9. He refused to take a young man who had deserted previously on a second missionary journey.
10. He refused in a vision to eat anything common or unclean.

(a) Peter
(b) Daniel
(c) Mordecai
(d) Uriah
(e) Naboth
(f) Jacob
(g) Laban
(h) Paul
(i) Elisha
(j) Pharaoh

23. The Gracious Ones

Below are a few of the many instances of acts of graciousness in the Bible. At the left are the "gracious ones." At the right are the things they did. How many can you match?

1. Paul
2. Lydia
3. Barnabas
4. Moses
5. Abraham
6. A captive maid
7. Rebekah
8. Ephron, for the sons of Heth
9. Three mighty men
10. Boaz

(a) Helped seven maidens who were driven away from the troughs they had filled
(b) Offered to let a kinsman take his choice of the land
(c) Offered water to a man, then to his camels
(d) Offered a man a cave for a burial place without price
(e) Offered hospitality to an apostle
(f) Spoke up for a man when others were hesitant about accepting him
(g) Expressed a wish that a certain prophet might cure a man — this led to the cure
(h) Broke through the enemy camp to get a man a drink from a certain well
(i) Told the workers in the field to let grain fall on purpose for a certain gleaner
(j) Wrote a letter to the owner of a fugitive slave in behalf of the slave

24. If

The title word had its place in Bible times, too. Each question is worth 10 points, if you do not refer to the list at the end of the quiz. If you choose the correct name from the list, it is worth 5 points. A score of 90-100 is excellent, 75-85 good, and 60-70 fair. If your score is less than 60 it's less than fair.

1. Who asked, "If a man die, shall he live again?"
2. Who told Jesus, "If thou hadst been here, my brother had not died."
3. Who decided to risk her life for her people, saying "If I perish, I perish."
4. Who promised the Lord if she should have a male child she would give that child to the Lord?
5. Who told the people, "If the Lord be God, follow him; but if Baal, then follow him."
6. Who told a woman he would go to take Sisera and his host if she would go with him?
7. Who said, "If God be for us, who can be against us?"
8. Who promised the Lord if he would deliver the Ammonites into his hands, he would offer the first thing that came to meet him from the house as a burnt offering?
9. Who told his father to slay his own two sons if he did not deliver his father's youngest son safe after a journey to Egypt?
10. Who worked out this code with his friend: If I say to the lad "The arrows are beyond you . . ." then go away, for your life is in danger.

Elijah	Paul	Reuben
Esther	Job	Hannah
Barak	Jonathan	Jephthah
	Martha	

25. Bible Crossword Puzzle in Numbers

The numbers are for the most part implied

ACROSS

1. Number of books in the Old Testament
3. Men in Gideon's Band (Judg. 7:7)
6. Number of books in the Bible
7. The shortest chapter is Psalm _____
9. Years Cainan lived (Gen. 5:14)
11. Chapters in I Chron. plus chapters in Matthew.
12. Number of Commandments
13. Number of days Joshua encompassed Jericho (Josh. 6:15)
14. Years Manasseh reigned (II Kings 21:1) plus chapters in Deuteronomy
15. Years the Israelites spent in the wilderness
16. Times Naaman washed in the Jordan (II Kings 5) times chapters in Micah
17. Number of cubits in the length of the temple plus the number in the height (I Kings 5:2)
18. Books of the Old Testament times Books of the New Testament times Books of the Bible

DOWN

1. Jacob's sons times Noah's sons
2. Years Methuselah lived
3. Chapters in Psalms times sons of Isaac times Commandments
4. Sons of Sarah
5. Solomon's proverbs (I Kings 4:32) divided by daughters of Laban
8. Years Lamech lived (Gen. 5:31)
10. The longest chapter is Psalm _____
14. Years Adam lived (Gen. 5:3) minus chapters in I Samuel
15. Chapters in Deuteronomy times the Disciples
16. Years David reigned (I Chron. 29:27) plus cities of refuge (Num. 35:6)
17. Sheep left in the fold (Matt. 18:12)
19. Number of Gospels

26. Read Down and Find

Fill in space 1. Drop one letter for space 2 and place the letter dropped in the box at the left. For space 3 drop another letter and place that letter in the box at the right. Fill in each row the same way. When you are through, read down the boxed letters, left and right, and find an answer Jesus gave two disciples. Philip later gave the same answer.

	1	2	3	
4	5	6		
7	8	9		
10	11	12		
13	14	15		

1. Son of Adam and Eve
2. Part of a boundary (Num. 34:11)
3. City of Ammon (Jer. 49:3)
4. Son of Ruth and Boaz
5. Place for rest (Job 7:13)
6. _____ strong (Josh. 1:18)
7. Son of Noah
8. Pronoun (Prov. 31:12)
9. Pronoun (Prov. 29:1)
10. Home of Adam and Eve
11. Lair (Job 37:8)
12. Debit note (abbr.)
13. Son of Adam and Eve
14. Babylonian idol (Isa. 46:1)
15. Bachelor of Letters (abbr.)

27. Crowded Line

In the line below there are names "crowded" so that the letters in one go over into those of another name. The names in the line are the names of the following people in the Bible, though not necessarily in the order given.

1. The head of a tribe
2. A king when Jesus was born
3. The first man
4. A woman who sheltered spies
5. A prophet
6. A great leader
7. A sister-in-law of the tetrarch
8. A queen who saved her people
9. The third king of Judah
10. The wife of a great patriarch
11. A son of Jether
12. A wicked king of Israel

GADAMOSESTHERODIASARAHAB

28. "And of the Prophets" . . . and Others

The eleventh chapter of Hebrews lists people of great faith, mentioning a number of names and ending the list with, "And of the prophets." Below are examples of prophets — and others in the Old Testament who evidenced great faith. How many names can you fill in?

1. _____ offered up a sacrifice on Mt. Carmel, defying the prophets of Baal.
2. _____ told Naaman to wash in the Jordan, knowing God would heal him.
3. _____ confronted David with his sin, saying, "Thou art the man."
4. _____ offered to interpret the king's dream if given time, feeling God would reveal the dream to him.
5. _____ went back to Jerusalem and rebuilt the wall.
6. _____, the high priest, watched over the hidden child Joash, for six years, then took steps to make him king.
7. _____ refused to yield to the king of Assyria and 185,000 Assyrians were slain in one night.
8. _____ went with Barak to fight Sisera, captain of the king of the Canaanite army.
9. _____ clung to his integrity, saying, "I know that my redeemer liveth."
10. _____, when she weaned her child, took him to the temple to be under the care of the priest.

29. They Changed

Below are instances in the Bible of people who changed, some over a period of years, others within a short time. Who are they?

1. He thrust prisoners into the inner prison, but later washed their stripes.
2. He persecuted the Christians, but later became an outstanding one.
3. He said he could not speak, but later he poured forth from his heart a song of deliverance.
4. She was a "woman with a past" but she hastened to tell her townsmen that Jesus was the Christ.
5. This young man turned back on his first missionary journey and was refused by Paul to accompany him on the second. Later, Paul asked for the young man.
6. He showed lack of courage after Jesus was taken in the Garden, but later was fearless in the face of persecution.
7. Because of lack of faith he wanted evidence, but later his faith paid Jesus the highest tribute when he cried, "My Lord and my God."
8. He seemed inclined to secrecy in coming to Jesus, but openly followed Him in His death and burial.
9. He had visions of being a powerful ruler, but when he was in high office he demonstrated great kindness and forgiveness.
10. He proposed selling a brother into slavery, but years later he offered to stay as hostage for another one.

30. Heavenly Space

The "heavens" have been given much consideration in this space age, but they were considered long ago, in Biblical times, not with reference to man's ability to go into space, but as the wonderful work of the Creator. Below are questions that give you one choice in three of choosing the right answer.

1. A command was given certain heavenly bodies by (a) Gideon, (b) Joshua, (c) Daniel
2. The command was (a) to stand still, (b) to shine more brightly, (c) to go down
3. They were (a) the moon and The Orion, (b) the sun and all the stars, (c) the sun and the moon
4. They (a) obeyed, (b) went on in their usual course, (c) obeyed for one minute
5. The constellation Ursa Major, or the great bear, is called by Job (a) Sirius, (b) Arcturus, (c) Vega
6. Job also mentions the constellation (a) Leo, (b) The Scales, (c) The Orion
7. The Orion is also mentioned by (a) Amos, (b) Isaiah, (c) no other Biblical writer
8. Job also mentions a group of stars known as (a) the Milky Way, (b) The Hyades, (c) The Pleiades
9. The Magi followed a Star which led them to (a) The City of Palms, (b) The Holy City, (c) The City of David
10. Astrology in Biblical times was (a) unknown, (b) known about but not practised, (c) practised
11. A writer who speaks of the glory of the heavenly bodies is (a) Luke, (b) Ezekiel, (c) Paul
12. God created the moon, "the lesser light to rule the night." Its light is (a) inherent, (b) refracted, (c) reflected

31. "The Unknown God"

In all but one line you are given letters in each of the words to be filled in. The letters in each line you fill in will form a word. When you are through, you will find, reading down the words you have filled in, a couplet about the "unknown god" Paul declares to the men of Athens.

_ _ H E R I T	Blessed are the meek; for they shall _____ the earth (Matt. 5:5)
_ _ _ S E L F	Joseph made _____ known (Gen. 45:1)
_ _ L F A R E	Well being (Neh. 2:10)
S _ _ _ _ R S	Splinters
M _ _ D F U L	Bearing in mind (Ps. 8:4)
S _ _ _ M E R	Flash
S _ _ E T E R	_____ also than the honey and the honeycomb (Ps. 19:10)
R E _ _ _ _ D	Remote (Gal. 1:6)
_ _ E P I N G	Rachel _____ for her children (Jer. 31:15)
_ _ _ D A C E	Queen of the Ethiopians (Acts 8:27)
_ _ _ H I N G	. . . and have not charity, I am _____ (I Cor. 13:2)
_ _ S P E L S	Writings of Matthew, Mark, Luke and John
_ _ _ _ _ _ _	Without (Judg. 7:11)
T _ _ _ T L E	Prickly plant (Gen. 3:18)
P _ _ _ _ R S	Shore birds

32. Both Rhyme and Reason

The words to be filled in rhyme with the words in italics at the right. There is a blank for each letter, and the words are the names of people with one exception.

1. _ _ _ _   The first king of Israel was *tall*
2. _ _ _ _   She told her mother-in-law the *truth*
3. _ _ _ _ _ _ _   She acted bravely, *lest her* people be destroyed
4. _ _ _ _   We should *hark* to his Gospel
5. _ _ _ _   His brother was *slain* by him
6. _ _ _ _ _ _   His wife was *Priscilla*
7. _ _ _   He *got* the better land, due to Abraham's generosity
8. _ _ _ _ _ _   She sheltered spies in Jericho before the time of *Ahab*
9. _ _ _ _   This book of the Bible is full of *facts* about the Apostles
10. _ _ _   This *man* was the son of Jacob
11. _ _ _   His *son* succeeded Moses
12. _ _ _ _ _ _ _   This mother of Samuel lived before *Anna* the prophetess

33. Read the Square Clockwise

The name from the Bible found in each of the numbered squares is to be filled in clockwise. For instance, $\begin{smallmatrix}MA\\KR\end{smallmatrix}$ would be MARK.

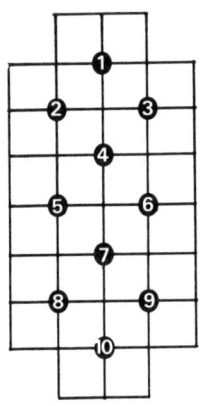

1. Son of Ham (Gen. 10:6)
2. King of Israel (I Kings 16:29)
3. Son of Noah
4. Prophet, also book of the Old Testament
5. Brother of Jacob
6. Son of Ruth and Boaz
7. Father of Abel
8. Father of Ahab (I Kings 16:29)
9. Prophetess (Luke 2:36)
10. A voice was heard here (Matt. 2:18)

34. Choice Within a Choice

You have one choice in three in the following numbers, but there is another choice in your answer — that of identifying the three people of the Bible given indirectly.

1. "I shot an arrow into the air." This act once had a special significance for (a) the strongest man, (b) the sweet singer of Israel, (c) The Father of the Faithful.
2. "Whither thou goest I will go," often sung at weddings, is from words uttered by (a) the sister of Moses, (b) the future wife of Elkanah, (c) the future mother of Obed.
3. Poe's most famous poem is about a bird. We associate the same bird with (a) a prophet, (b) a priest, (c) a king.
4. "The Assyrian came down like the wolf on the fold," said Byron, referring to a great deliverance in the reign of (a) the twelfth king of Judah, (b) the second king of Israel, (c) Herod the Tetrarch.
5. The story of Androcles brings to mind the beast we associate with four youths in (a) Moab, (b) Egypt, (c) Babylon.
6. "Under the willow, the gray." One of the Psalms tells of harps hung upon willows by the weeping (a) Hebrews returning from Babylon, (b) Moabites scattered along the way, (c) Philistines in Canaan.
7. "To George Washington, the _____ of America, who commanded the sun and the moon to stand still — and they obeyed" is a famous toast. The blank should be filled with the name of (a) the son of Zebedee, (b) the son son of Elah, (c) the son of Num.
8. We hear the expression, "He'll never turn the world upside down." Accused of doing this were (a) a couple of missionaries, (b) a silversmith and his wife, (c) two of the twelve disciples.

35. "Frustrations" in the Bible

In Bible times as well as today things seemed to go wrong, though they sometimes turned out right. Below are a few illustrations. Answer as many as you can without looking at the list below. 9 points for each correct identification. If you choose the correct one after looking at the list, 7 points. A score of 90 is excellent, 70 good, but below 60 is "a bit frustrating."

1. He could not enter the Promised Land he had made a long journey for.
2. He wanted to build a temple, but his reign was too full of war.
3. He sulked when a city was not destroyed he had prophesied would be.
4. This judge well might — though he won the fight — ask, "What price victory?"
5. When their brother was ill they called for One — but death was the first to come.
6. She and her son were sent away, and the wilderness was their home.
7. Famine drove her to Moab's land where she lost her mate and sons.
8. He was a great and righteous judge, though his sons were unworthy ones.
9. The girl of his life became his wife — after years of work had sped.
10. Though this prophet was brave he lodged in a cave — from a wicked queen he fled.
11. Two took their stand for taking the land — but the rest of them would stay.
12. Rome was the goal of this stalwart soul — he was shipwrecked on the way.

Eli	Jacob	Elijah
Moses	David	Jonah
Hagar	Paul	Caleb and Joshua
Jephthah	Naomi	Mary and Martha

36. Archaeological Discoveries

Below are instances of archaeological discoveries, and at the right are names which should go in the blanks. How many can you place correctly?

1. One today may look upon the actual face of the Pharaoh that had dealings with _____.
2. In Jericho have been found ruins of double walls linked together by houses, like that of _____.
3. In Megiddo ruins of stables have been discovered, stables undoubtedly belonging to _____.
4. Running seventeen hundred feet through solid rock was the tunnel of _____, which has been discovered.
5. A school room was found in Ur, probably the one in which young _____ studied.
6. In Megiddo were found jars containing the remains of infants sacrificed to Baal, whose prophets were challenged by _____.
7. Ruins of ancient Nineveh have been identified, and one of the mounds is called the _____ mound.
8. The site of Shushan, 200 miles east of Babylon, has been identified. This was the palace of _____.
9. The ruins of an ivory palace have been discovered, the palace belonging to _____.
10. The foundation of a wall has been found — the wall upon which handwriting was interpreted by _____.

(a) Daniel
(b) Ahab
(c) Moses
(d) Solomon
(e) Jonah
(f) Ahasuerus
(g) Rahab
(h) Elijah
(i) Abraham
(j) Hezekiah

37. "Now the Day Is Over"

1. When the sun was going down a deep sleep fell upon _____. He was told his seed would be in a strange land for four hundred years.

2. The sun was set, and he lay down, a stone for a pillow, and dreamed of a ladder.

3. "Abide with us," they told the risen Lord, "for the day is far spent." Can you give the name of one?

4. He went out to meditate in the field at eventide and saw his future wife approaching. Who was he?

5. At the time of the evening sacrifice a prophet prayed that the sacrifice to God, upon which water had been poured, would be consumed. Who was he?

6. When the sun was setting people with various diseases were brought to Jesus. How many were healed?

7. At eventide Jesus came when the doors were closed and said, "Peace be unto you." Who was in the room?

8. When it was evening a great multitude was fed. With what?

9. It was dark when a woman told pursuers of two spies she was sheltering, to hasten that they might find the spies. Who was she?

10. At a supper in Bethany sat a man whom Jesus had raised from the dead. Who was he?

38. Word Acrostic

When you have filled in the blanks arrange the letters according to their numbers in the diagram below. You will have a command given the children of Israel. The first row of letters of the words filled in will, reading down, give another name for "kinsman."

1D	2A	3D		4I	5B		6I	7H	8H
9C	10G		11A	12I	13E	14E	15D	16H	
17D	18I	19I	20B	21C		22H	23B	24I	
25H	26G	27I	28G		29E	30C	31E		
			32F	33A	34D	35F	36C	37G	

A. ___ ___ ___
  11 33 2
... and his father saw him, ... and _____, and fell on his neck (Luke 15:20)

B. ___ ___ ___
  5 23 20
... a liar giveth _____ to a naughty tongue (Prov. 17:4)

C. ___ ___ ___ ___
  36 30 9 21
The _____ of the valley

D. ___ ___ ___ ___ ___
  1 15 34 17 3
... he goeth on to meet the _____ men (Job 39:21)

E. ___ ___ ___ ___
  13 29 14 31
In this or that manner

F. ___ ___
  35 32
___ ye love me, keep my commandments (John 14:15)

G. ___ ___ ___ ___
  28 26 10 37
... and I, even I _____, am left (I Kings 19:14)

H. ___ ___ ___ ___ ___
  16 8 7 25 22
Prophet and book of the Old Testament

I. ___ ___ ___ ___ ___ ___ ___
  6 12 18 19 24 27 4
Until _____ times seven (Matt. 18:22)

39. Square of Squares

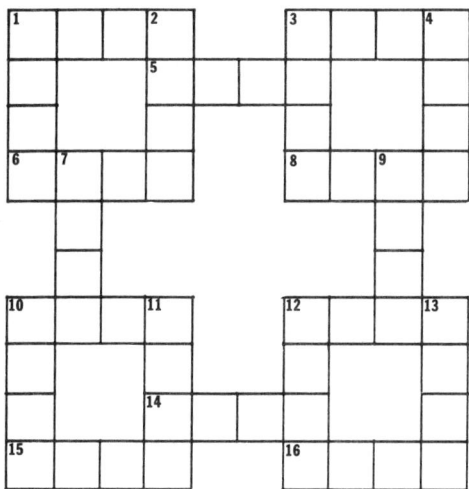

ACROSS

1. Son of Adam and Eve
3. Ruth's native land
5. Book of the Old Testament
6. Son of Zopath (I Chron. 7:36)
8. King of Judah (II Kings 15:38)
10. Book of the New Testament
12. Zoar (Gen. 14:2)
14. A prophetess (Luke 2:36)
15. Father of Ham
16. Timothy's grandmother (II Tim. 1:5)

DOWN

1. Wicked king of Israel
2. Son of Jacob
3. What Naomi said to call her (Ruth 1:20)
4. He married Ruth
7. Son of Isaac
9. Brother of Cain
10. Book of the New Testament
11. Valley in which David slew Goliath (I Sam. 17:19)
12. Heathen god
13. Book of the Old Testament

40. On the Way

Below are Biblical occurrences that happened "on the way" from one place to another. How many can you match?

1. Jesus was met by a crowd who waved branches and cried, "Blessed is he that cometh in the name of the Lord."
2. Paul was converted.
3. The Good Samaritan helped a man who had been robbed.
4. Paul was shipwrecked.
5. Samson killed a lion.
6. The children of Israel wandered forty years in the wilderness.
7. Philip saw a eunuch, explained the Scriptures to him, and later baptized him.
8. Jacob had a vision of angels ascending and descending.
9. Jesus appeared to two after the resurrection.
10. Lot's wife was turned to a pillar of salt.
11. Jacob's sons found a cup in Benjamin's sack.
12. Jesus rebuked the water, and there was a calm.

(a) On the way to Rome
(b) On the way to Timnath, to marry a Philistine
(c) On the way to Padan-aram
(d) On the way to Damascus
(e) On the way to Jericho, from Jerusalem
(f) On the way to Emmaus
(g) On the way to Zoar, fleeing from Sodom
(h) On the way to Jerusalem
(i) On the way to the country of the Gadarenes.
(j) On the way to Canaan, the Promised Land
(k) On the way to Gaza
(l) On the way home to Canaan

45

41. Find the Proverb

Begin with the upper left square and move in any direction to any adjacent square, and spell a well-known truth in Proverbs. All of the letters are used, but no letter more than one time.

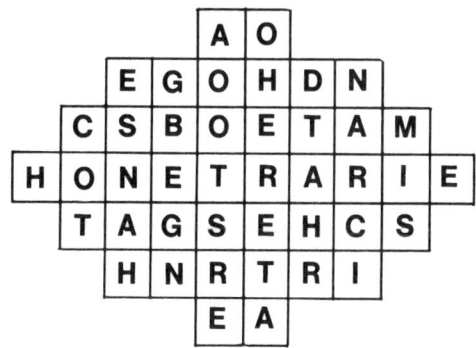

42. Featuring Food

1. Who would not dine on meat and wine but ate simple pulse instead?
2. Who paid his brother a mighty price for the pottage on which he fed?
3. Who stopped at a woman's house for bread whenever he passed that way?
4. Who gathered fresh food from the ground — enough for their need each day?
5. Who filled his brothers' sacks with corn in time of famine and stress?
6. Who ate wild honey and locusts? (His was a voice in the wilderness)
7. Who stayed with a woman and her son, when many a meal they got
   From a cruse of oil that did not fail and a barrel that wasted not?
8. What poor man ate of the crumbs that fell from a rich man's sumptuous fare?
9. Who with five fishes and two loaves fed a crowd, with much to spare?
10. For whom was killed a fatted calf when he turned his footsteps home?
    Unwelcomed by one, an elder brother who had never tried roam?
11. Who, when drinking wine from a vessel of gold, saw writing that made him fear?
12. Who wished to own for a garden of herbs a vineyard lying near?

43. Bird, Beast, and Insect

Supposing they could talk, how many of the following imagined lines can you match?

1. I helped feed a prophet at the Lord's command.
2. I brought back a welcome sign of land.
3. The sluggard is told to consider my ways.
4. I was one of the plagues in Pharaoh's days.
5. A brave young man was unharmed by me.
6. I left Absalom caught by a great oak tree.
7. I was used in a riddle a strong man made.
8. I ate the gourd that was Jonah's shade.
9. When even I fall the Father knows.
10. I was one of a dream where the long Nile flows.

(a) Ant
(b) Mule
(c) Cow
(d) Locust
(e) Lion
(f) Raven
(g) Sparrow
(h) Bee
(i) Worm
(j) Dove

44. Triple Proportion

In each of the numbers below there is one proportion that is incorrect. Which one is it?

1. Samson is to strong as Abraham is to faithful as Moses is to bold
2. Deborah is to judge as Esther is to deaconess as Anna is to prophetess
3. Hannah is to Samuel as Lois is to Timothy as Rachel is to Benjamin
4. Naomi is to Ruth as Sarah is to Rebekah as Hagar is to Ishmael
5. Esau is to hunter as Paul is to tent-maker as Cain is to shepherd
6. Disciples is to twelve as deacons is to fourteen as commandments is to ten
7. Joshua is to Kish as David is to Jesse as Obed is to Boaz
8. Elah is to valley as Jordan is to river as Nebo is to brook
9. Genesis is to law as Exodus is to going out as Psalms is to hymns
10. James is to John as David is to Jonathan as Peter is to Andrew
11. Martha is to Bethany as Lydia is to Thyatira as Rahab is to Corinth

45. Acrostic

R _ _ _ _ _	She was loved by Jacob
_ E _ _ _ _	Jacob's oldest son
_ _ A _ _ _	Prophet — book of the Old Testament
_ _ _ D _ _	John baptized Jesus in this river
_ _ _ _ T _	Descendant of the "priestly tribe"
_ _ _ _ H _	Jesus visited at her home in Bethany
_ _ _ _ E _	Jewish queen who saved her people
_ _ _ _ B' _	Whose brother was Esau?
_ _ _ I _ _	She watched over her baby brother
_ _ B _ _ _	He had a vineyard the king coveted
_ L _ _ _ _	Fruit of Palestine (pl.)
E _ _ _ _ _	He challenged the prophets of Baal
_ E _ _ _ _	Moses' father-in-law
_ _ V _ _ _	Jesus is our _____
_ _ _ E _ _	The _____ and nine
_ _ _ _ R' _	Whose brother was Andrew?
_ _ _ _ Y' _	What animal's name is among those forbidden? (Deut. 14:7)
_ _ _ D _ _	The _____ of Eden
_ _ A _ _ _	A leper who washed in the river Jordan
_ Y _ _ _ _	Paul and Barnabas fled to this city

46. How Many?

There are 10 Commandments, 27 Books in the New Testament, and 12 Disciples. Below you are to give numbers as answers. Some answers are duplicated. If your own numbers are correct, they should total 1466.

HOW MANY:

_____ 1. Books in the Bible?

_____ 2. Verses in the shortest chapter?

_____ 3. Sons of Jacob?

_____ 4. Men did Gideon choose to fight the Midianites?

_____ 5. Days did Joshua compass the city of Jericho?

_____ 6. Plagues were visited on the Egyptians?

_____ 7. Sons had Noah?

_____ 8. Years did Methuselah live?

_____ 9. Years were the children of Israel in the wilderness?

_____ 10. Books in the Pentateuch?

_____ 11. Years did Jacob work for Laban?

_____ 12. Major prophets?

_____ 13. Minor prophets?

_____ 14. Birds did Noah send from the ark?

_____ 15. Deacons were first appointed?

_____ 16. Times did Peter deny Jesus?

_____ 17. Horsemen did John write about in *Revelation*?

_____ 18. Churches in Asia does John address in *Revelation*?

1466

47. The Parables

Each verse or excerpt at the right should bring to mind the Parable it is taken from. The Parables are at the left.

1. The Laborers in the Vineyard
2. The Sower
3. The Merciless Servant
4. The Tares
5. The Rich Fool
6. The Good Samaritan
7. The Mustard Seed
8. The Good Shepherd
9. The Lost Sheep
10. The Prodigal Son
11. The Great Supper
12. The Ten Virgins
13. The Talents
14. The Pharisee and the Publican
15. The Wicked Husbandman
16. The Barren Fig Tree

(a) And when he saw him, he passed by on the other side
(b) And they all with one consent began to make excuses
(c) Give us of your oil; for our lamps are gone out
(d) So the last shall be first, and the first shall be last
(e) I fast twice in the week, I give tithes of all that I possess
(f) Let both grow together until the harvest
(g) And when he hath found it, he layeth it on his shoulders
(h) Have patience with me, and I will pay thee all
(i) And yet thou never gavest me a kid, that I might make merry with my friends
(j) Some fell upon stony places
(k) Lord, let it alone this year also, till I shall dig about it
(l) It grew, and waxed a great tree
(m) Other sheep have I, which are not of this fold
(n) Eat, drink, and be merry
(o) But last of all he sent unto them his son, saying, they will reverence my son
(p) For unto every one that hath shall be given, and he shall have abundance

48. Who?

1. Who was the most patient man? Who was the strongest?
2. Who was the wisest? Whose life was the longest?
3. Who "was not" for God took him? Who was cast in the sea?
4. Who begged a ruler to set his people free?
5. Who for his crime had no home on the earth?
6. Who refused to return to the place of her birth?
7. Who was Judah's first king? Who was Israel's last?
8. Who befriended a poor man whom others had passed?
9. Who thrice suffered shipwreck? Who acted as a spy?
10. Who heard the Lord's voice and said, "Here am I"?
11. Who had a vision in which was a sheet?
12. Who, cast in a furnace, suffered not from the heat?
13. Who played the harp and wrote many a psalm?
14. Who spoke the wind and waves into calm?
15. Who asked a question of Jesus by night?
16. Who climbed a tree — for short was his height?
17. Who made a coat for a favorite son?
18. Who with three hundred men a great victory won?

49. "Dare to Be a Daniel"

D _ _ _ _ _ _	Nebuchadnezzar did this (Dan. 2:1)
A _ _ _ _ _ _	One of Daniel's friends (Dan. 1:6)
R _ _ _ _ _ _	Declined. Daniel _____ to eat the king's meat
E _ _ _ _ _ _	The _____ God is thy refuge (Deut. 33:27)
T _ _ _ _ _ _	Shake with fear (Dan. 6:26)
O _ _ _ _ _ _	. . . for man looketh on the _____ appearance (I Sam. 16:7)
B _ _ _ _ _ _	Where Daniel lived in exile
E _ _ _ _ _ _	Foes (Dan. 4:19)
A _ _ _ _ _ _	Refrain voluntarily, as Daniel did
D _ _ _ _ _ _	Set free (Dan. 3:17)
A _ _ _ _ _ _	Power (Dan. 1:4)
N _ _ _ _ _ _	What happened to Daniel in the den of lions?
I _ _ _ _ _ _	Blessed are the meek: for they shall _____ the earth
E _ _ _ _ _ _	Daniel is a good _____ of steadfastness and courage
L _ _ _ _ _ _	Freedom (Ps. 119:45)

50. Quote — Misquote

There are many references to the Bible in literature. Below are a few excerpts, some of which are quoted correctly. Others are misquoted. If you can identify them, can you correct them?

1. Rose on the ardor of prayer, like Elisha ascending to heaven.   — *Longfellow*
2. How bloody Pharaoh slew the innocents.   — *Browning*
3. What is truth? asked jesting Herod, and would not stay for an answer.   — *Lord Bacon*
4. One was the Tishbite whom the eagles fed.   — *Tennyson*
5. Ah! broken is the golden bowl!   — *Poe*
6. I am as poor as Job, my lord; but not so patient.   — *Shakespeare*
7. "May the wheels of their chariots be taken off," said the Jew, "like those of the host of Ahab."   — *Sir Walter Scott*
8. Gentlemen may cry "Peace, Peace" — but there is no peace.   — *Patrick Henry*
9. Who know with John his smile of love,
   With Matthew his rebuke.   — *Whittier*
10. Contrary to Joshua's miracle, while all around were drenched, our fleece was dry.   — *Lamb*
11. And here one master passion in the breast
    Like Aaron's serpent, swallows up the rest.   — *Pope*
12. Like unto shipwrecked Paul on Melita's desolate seashore.   — *Longfellow*

51. Sally's Complaint

How many expressions of Sally's are rooted in the Bible?

Said Sally, "My boy friend and I
Just can not see things eye to eye.
I don't say he has feet of clay —
He's rather super in a way —
Although he'll never go to town
In turning the world upside down.
Our war of nerves is grating, for
There is no discharge in that war.
We can be secure, I say,
By putting something by each day.
A little here, a little there,
And we will have enough to spare.
But no, he wants to do things big.
His spending sprees I just don't dig.
As ravenous as a wolf we'll be
Unless he learns economy."

52. "Judge" for Yourself

From the journey through the wilderness to the time of Saul the Israelites were for the most part ruled by judges. The numbers below include the most outstanding ones, and you are to "judge for yourself" in matching them with the names at the right. However, a good score probably shows more knowledge than judgment.

1. He slew more in death than he had in his life.
2. His rule was a long one and one free from strife.
3. He marched round a city, and down came the wall.
4. His wife's father said to quit doing it all.
5. They wanted a king, and it made his heart sad.
6. Each son ruled a city — and thirty he had.
7. This left-handed judge slew a Moabite king.
8. An ode of triumph this judge helped to sing.
9. His vow was a rash one, yet he felt honor-bound.
10. He saw the dry fleece upon dewy-wet ground.

(a) Joshua
(b) Gideon
(c) Samuel
(d) Othniel
(e) Jair
(f) Jephthah
(g) Deborah
(h) Samson
(i) Moses
(j) Ehud

53. The Nameless Ones

There are many people in the Bible whose names are not given, but they are remembered just the same. Below are instances, and you are to match the two columns. If you match eight or more you are among those that remember well.

1. One of the lepers
2. A captive maid
3. Paul's nephew
4. A woman of Samaria
5. A woman of Canaan
6. A lad
7. A eunuch of Ethiopia
8. The eldest servant
9. Jephthah's daughter
10. A Shunammite

(a) was told by Jesus that her faith was great
(b) furnished the loaves and fishes for Jesus to feed the multitude
(c) found a wife for Isaac
(d) gave her life so that a vow might not be broken
(e) was instrumental in Naaman's cure
(f) told of a plot
(g) was an early Gentile convert
(h) returned to thank Jesus
(i) talked with Jesus at the well
(j) made a room ready for Elisha

54. "Name" the Italics

You are asked to discover the twelve people in the Bible whose names contain the italicized letters below, one name to a line of verse. Each line also contains a clue.

1. He had *a use* for a hunter's free life.
2. Not at *Elah* lived Jacob's first wife.
3. *Ah, robed* in justice, a judge was she.
4. *O a balm's* not the fruit of his fateful tree.
5. Was *a shoe* or sandal this prophet's footgear?
6. No *lie* told Hannah to this priest who was near.
7. *Omit thy* mother and grandmother? Nay!
8. Did his dad have *a brahma* in Ur on display?
9. What was *'e doin*g with three hundred men?
10. He was no *warden* but a fisherman then.
11. A *quail* isn't mentioned in this tentmaker's fare.
12. Paul goes to Rome. He *sails* not with him there.

55. Down the Alphabet

A is for _ _ _ _, the father of Cain,
B is for _ _ _ _, who had fields of grain,
C is for _ _ _ _ _, a courageous spy,
D is for _ _ _ _ _ _, who a needle did ply,
E is for _ _ _ _ _ _, a queen beauty was she,
F is for _ _ _ _ _, to whom Paul made a plea,
G is for _ _ _ _ _ _, known for his sword,
H is for _ _ _ _ _ _, brought her child to the Lord,
I is for _ _ _ _ _, Sarah, his mother,
J is for _ _ _ _ _ _, Benjamin's brother,
K is for _ _ _ _, the father of Saul,
L is for _ _ _ _ _, converted by Paul,
M is for _ _ _ _ _, found by Pharaoh's daughter,
N is for _ _ _ _, whose ark stood the water,
O is for _ _ _ _ _, back to Moab she went,
P is for _ _ _ _, to Rome he was sent,
Q is for _ _ _ _ _ _ _, whom Paul briefly mentions,
R is for _ _ _ _, filled her loyal intentions,
S is for _ _ _ _ _ _, a strong man was he,
T is for _ _ _ _, who said he must see,
U is for _ _ _ _ _, in battle "effaced,"
V is for _ _ _ _ _ _, by Esther replaced,
No names with W, X, Y we can see,
Z's for _ _ _ _ _ _ _ _ _, climbed a sycamore tree.

56. This Is _ _ _ _ _ _ Speaking

"This is Cora, Cora, C as in Carl, O as in Opal, R as in Reba, and A as in Anne," said Cora over the telephone when she was having trouble in making her identity known. Assuming there were telephones in Biblical days, can you identify the assumed Biblical characters speaking, from similar clues — you will have to be familiar with the "clues" and identify them as well.

Granted there were telephones then, still one conversation would have been impossible. Can you tell why?

1. This is _ _ _ _ _ _:
__ as in the first king of Israel, __ as in Abraham's son, __ as in the father of Rachel, __ as in Moses' spokesman, and __ as in the wisest man.

2. This is _ _ _ _ _ _:
__ as in either of Lazarus' sisters, __ as in the slave Paul wrote about, __ as in Paul's fellow prisoner in Philippi, __ as in the brother of Jacob and __ as in the first Christian martyr.

3. This is _ _ _ _ _ _:
__ as in "The Apostle," __ as in the mother of Abel, __ as in the father of Abraham, __ as in the father of Hophni and Phinehas, and __ as in the wife of Boaz.

4. This is _ _ _ _ _:
__ as in the sister of Rachel, __ as in the son of Ruth, __ as in the son of Rebekah, and __ as in the last judge.

5. This is _ _ _ _ _ _:
__ as in "The Dreamer" of Jacob's sons, __ as in David's handsome son, __ as in the Hebrew law-giver, __ as in Samuel's father and __ as in Abraham's wife.

57. They Were "Human"

One thing that makes many of the characters in the Bible seem so real is the account of their "human" traits that creep out in family relationships. Can you identify the characters in the instances below?

1. She complained to the Guest for whom she was preparing a meal that her sister was letting her do most of the work.
2. Many mothers help their daughters make a good marriage, but this mother-in-law did it for her daughter-in-law after her son was dead. However, the daughter-in-law had proved her loyalty.
3. She maneuvered to get her favorite son the blessing that belonged to his brother, and she saw that her favorite escaped the cheated brother's anger.
4. He was a great man and a great leader, but his father-in-law told him he was working too hard and needed help. He took the advice.
5. There was contention between the herdsmen of a nephew and his uncle, and when told by the uncle to take his choice of the land he chose the more fruitful site.
6. He made his sons judges as he had been — but they failed to qualify as he had done.
7. When he was seventeen he was herding the flocks with his elder brothers, and when he came home he "told on them."
8. This father, a good Priest, did not restrain his two sons, who brought him grief.
9. This youth began asking questions about the enemy, and his oldest brother, suspecting he had in mind volunteering to fight him single-handedly, asked him with whom he had left the sheep — why he had come.
10. His grief at the death of his foe was great — for his enemy was his son.

58. What Were They Doing?

Many Biblical characters were engaged in doing commonplace things when they had experiences that made great changes in their lives. Some of the things were not so commonplace. Below are a few instances.

1. What was Paul doing when he had the great experience on the way to Damascus?
2. What were Peter and Andrew doing when Jesus called them to be his disciples?
3. What was Rebekah doing when she was chosen to be the wife of Isaac?
4. What was Saul doing when he decided to consult Samuel — which resulted in his being anointed king?
5. What was David doing when he was sent for, and anointed?
6. What was Moses doing when God told him to go to Egypt and set free his people?
7. What was Jacob doing when he had the vision of the ladder, and received God's blessing?
8. What was Elisha doing when Elijah cast his mantle upon Elisha's shoulders?
9. What was Matthew doing when he was called to be a disciple?
10. What was Joseph doing when Pharaoh sent for him to interpret a dream?
11. What was Gideon doing when an angel appeared to him?

59. Questions in the Bible (Part 1)

Below are questions found in the Bible. At the right are the persons asking them. How many can you match?

1. Simon, son of Jonas, lovest thou me?
2. Am I my brother's keeper?
3. Lord, we know not whither thou goest; and how can we know the way?
4. Doth my father yet live?
5. If a man die, shall he live again?
6. Where is he that is born King of the Jews?
7. Lord, dost thou not care that my sister hath left me to serve alone?
8. Is there no balm in Gilead?
9. O death, where is thy sting? O grave, where is thy victory?
10. What is man, that thou art mindful of him?
11. Shall I and thy mother and thy brethren indeed come to bow ourselves to thee to the earth?
12. ... and who knoweth whether thou art come to the kingdom for such a time as this?
13. Understandest thou what thou readest?
14. Behold the fire and the wood; but where is the lamb for a burnt offering?
15. Is it lawful to give tribute unto Caesar, or not?

(a) Jeremiah
(b) Martha
(c) Jacob
(d) Philip
(e) David
(f) Isaac
(g) Mordecai
(h) Thomas
(i) Pharisees
(j) Jesus
(k) St. Paul
(l) Wise men from the east
(m) Cain
(n) Joseph
(o) Job

60. Questions in the Bible — Part 2

Below are more questions found in the Bible. At the right are the persons asking them. How many can you match?

1. What is truth?
2. Can any good thing come out of Nazareth?
3. Is the young man Absalom safe?
4. How can a man be born when he is old?
5. Why was not this ointment sold for three hundred pence, and given to the poor?
6. Good master, what good thing shall I do, that I may inherit eternal life?
7. ... is thy God, whom thou servest continually, able to deliver thee from the lions?
8. And who is my neighbor?
9. Who am I, that I should go unto Pharaoh and that I should bring forth the children of Israel out of Egypt?
10. If God be for us, who can be against us?
11. Can two walk together, except they be agreed?
12. ... when shall these things be? And what shall be the sign when all these things shall be fulfilled?
13. Who hath believed our report?
14. Is not this great Babylon, that I have built for the house of my kingdom?
15. What meanest the bleating of sheep ... and the lowing of the oxen which I hear?

(a) Amos
(b) St. Paul
(c) The rich young ruler
(d) Peter, James, John and Andrew
(e) Isaiah
(f) Moses
(g) Samuel
(h) Judas Iscariot
(i) Nebuchadnezzar
(j) A certain lawyer
(k) Darius
(l) Nicodemus
(m) David
(n) Nathanael
(o) Pilate

ANSWERS

1. Mothers in the Bible

1(l)	Gen. 29	7(r)	I Sam. 1
2(m)	Gen. 21	8(a)	Gen. 4:1
3(j)	Ruth 3	9(d)	II Sam. 12:24
4(n)	Gen. 21:14	10(p)	Gen. 37:3 & 44:20
5(i)	Josh. 2:4	11(e)	Luke 1:41
6(q)	Matt. 1	12(c)	II Kings 4:8-34

13(f) Mark 15:40; Matt. 27:56
14(b) II Kings 9:30-33
15(h) II Kings 11:1
16(g) Judg. 4:4
17(o) Gen. 27
18(k) II Tim. 1:5

2. Imaginary Greeting to Mother

1(g)	3(b)	5(h)	7(f)	9(j)
2(a)	4(i)	6(d)	8(e)	10(c)

3. Double Match in Relationships

1-f-I   (I Sam. 9:1-2, I Sam. 19:1)
2-h-F   (Gen. 43:26-29, Gen. 46:20)
3-a-D   (Exod. 4:18, Exod. 6:20)
4-c-A   (Gen. 24:67, Gen. 29:28, Gen. 30:22-24, Gen. 41:51)
5-j-C   (Gen. 21:3, Gen. 11:31)
6-b-G   (Gen. 29:10-12, Gen. 25:20-26, Gen. 37:3)
7-i-B   (II Tim. 1:5)
8-e-H   (Matt. 4:21)
9-d-J   (Matt. 1:5 [Rachab, Greek form of Rahab] Ruth 4:13-17)
10-g-E   (Gen. 5:3, Gen. 5:6)

4. The Elder Brother (or Sister)

1. Aaron and Moses (Exod. 4:10-16)
2. Esau and Jacob (Gen. 27:41)
3. James and John (Acts 12:2; Revelation of St. John the Divine)
4. Eliab and David (I Sam. 17:28)
5. Joseph and Benjamin (Gen. 45:14)
6. Leah and Rachel (Gen. 29:26)
7. Manasseh and Ephraim (Gen. 48:17-19)
8. Cain and Abel (Gen. 4:4-5)
9. Joel and Abiah (I Sam. 8:2-3)
10. Martha and Mary (John 11:28)

5. Brothers in the Square

1. Esau
2. Laban
3. Andrew
4. Benjamin
5. Lazarus
6. Moses
7. Ephraim
8. Japheth
9. Abel
10. Hophni
11. James

6. Making Names of Names

1. Jo—Nathan, Jonathan
2. Dan—iel, Daniel
3. Sus—Anna, Susanna (Luke 8:3)
4. Sam – Uel, Samuel (Ezra 10:34)
5. Herod—ias, Herodias (Matt. 14:3)
6. Jo – Shua, Joshua (1 Chron. 2:3)
7. Zippor—ah, Zipporah (Num. 22:2)
8. Bath—Sheba, (Bathsheba (II Sam. 20:1)
9. Ham—an, Haman (Esther 3:8)
10. Eli—jah, Elijah

7. Featuring Four-letter Names in the Bible

1. M A R K
   A V O N
   R O S E
   K N E W

2. A D A M
   D I M E
   A M E N
   M E N D

3. A M O S
   M A K E
   O K R A
   S E A M

4. L E A H
   E Z R A
   A R A M
   H A M E

5. J O H N
   O L E O
   H E N A
   N O A H

6. L O I S
   O U S T
   I S L E
   S T E P

8. Much in a Name

1. Seth (Gen. 4:25)
2. Moses (Exod. 2:10)
3. Gad (Gen. 30:11)
4. Samuel (I Sam. 1:20)
5. Ephraim (Gen. 41:52)
6. Gershom (Exod. 2:22)
7. Joseph (Gen. 30:22-24)
8. Solomon (II Sam. 12:24)
9. John (Luke 1:59-62)
10. Esau (Gen. 25:25)

9. Relatives

1. mother, Rachel (Gen. 30:22-24; 35:15-18)
2. grandfather, Jacob (Gen. 46:19-20)
3. sister, Martha (John 11:1)
4. son, Timothy (II Tim. 1:5)
5. mother, Jochebed (Num. 26:59)
6. father, Zebedee (Matt. 10:2)
7. mother, Ruth (Ruth 4:13-17)
8. wife, Hannah (I Sam. 1:1-20)
9. grandson, Lot (Gen. 11:31)
10. sister, Rebekah (Gen. 29:10)

10. Fathers and Mothers

1(g) Eunice (II Tim. 1:5)
2(l) (I Sam. 13:22)
3(h) Athaliah (II Kings 11:1)
4(j) Joseph (Gen. 41:49; 41:52)

5(i)   Moses (Exod. 8:24; 2:21-22)
6(k)   Rahab (Gr. for, Rachab, Matt. 1:5; Josh. 2)
7(b)   Ruth (Ruth 2:17; 4:17)
8(e)   Abraham (Gen. 11:31; 21:3)
9(c)   Jacob (Gen. 27)
10(f) Bathsheba (II Sam. 11; 12:24)
11(d) Hannah (I Sam. 1:20; 1:25)
12(a) Solomon (I Kings 11:43; Prov. 12:10)

11. Also — One of Three

1(a)   I Kings 11:42
2(b)   Acts 18:2-3
3(b)   Gen. 39:6
4(c)
5(a)   Luke 19:2 (publican)
6(c)   Acts 10:9-12
7(c)   I Sam. 1:3
8(c)   Exod. 15
9(c)   Acts 14:12
10(b) Matt. 1:5 (Gr. form of name)
11(c) Gen. 21
12(b) Gen. 48

12. Hidden Names

1. David
2. Obed
3. Andrew
4. Silas
5. Leah
6. Lois
7. Esther
8. Lydia
9. Paul
10. Esau
11. Samson
12. Eli

13. "Thank You" Notes

1. To my sister Miriam
   From Moses (Exod. 2:4, 7)
2. To my mother-in-law Naomi
   From Ruth (Ruth 3)
3. To my nephew (unnamed)
   From Paul (Acts 23:16)
4. To my friend Jonathan
   From David (I Sam. 20)
5. To my Uncle Abraham
   From Lot (Gen. 13:8-12)
6. To my Cousin Mordecai
   From Esther (Esther 2:5-17)

14. Descriptive Words

1. Beautiful . . good Isa. 52:7)
2. Broken . . contrite (Ps. 51:17)
3. Wise . . glad . . foolish (Prov. 15:20)
4. Lovely . . pleasant (II Sam. 1:23)
5. Silver . . golden (Eccles. 12:6)
6. Faithful . . just (I John 1:9)
7. Kind . . tenderhearted (Eph. 4:32)
8. Wise . . harmless (Matt. 10:16)
9. Sweet . . bitter (James 3:11)
10. Easy . . light (Matt. 11:30)
11. Perfect . . sure . . wise (Ps. 19:7)
12. Perverse . . crooked (Deut. 32:5)
13. Green . . still (Ps. 23:2)
14. Soft . . grievous (Prov. 15:1)
15. Swift . . strong (Eccles. 9:11)

15. Songs from the Bible

1(e)	Acts 3:8	7(l)	Acts 26:28
2(i)	Exod. 12:12	8(f)	I Sam. 7:12
3(k)	Isa. 6:8	9(c)	John 3:2
4(j)	I John 5:4	10(a)	Exod. 33:22
5(h)	Gen. 28:12	11(d)	Dan. 3:17
6(b)	Rev. 6:16	12(g)	Mal. 3:17

16. "What Time I Am Afraid"

1. Elijah (I Kings 19:3)
2. Nehemiah (Neh. 2:2)
3. David (I Sam. 20)
4. Moses (Exod. 2:11-14)
5. Jacob (Gen. 27:27, 41)
6. Joseph's brothers (Gen. 44:12-13)
7. Esther (Esther 4:16)
8. Hezekiah (II Chron. 32:20)
9. The keeper of the prison (Acts 16:27-29)
10. Lot (Gen. 19:30)
11. Peter (Luke 22:57)
12. Spies (Num. 13)

17. Biblical Proportions

1. Boaz
2. Meek
3. Daniel
4. "Rock"
5. Twelve
6. Tax collector
7. Seller of purple
8. Sea
9. Height or mountain
10. Harp
11. Zedekiah
12. Solomon
13. Genesis, Exodus, Leviticus, Numbers and Deuteronomy
14. Jacob
15. **Rachel**
16. Babylon
17. Tishbite
18. Wisdom

18. Paul

1(a)
2(b)
3(a) Saul
4(c) Stephen
5(c)
6(c)
7(b)
8(a)
9(b)
10(a)
11(b)
12(c)
13(c)
14(c)

19. A Question of Concern

Is the young man Absalom safe?
(Reading Down) His Son
Ham's
If
Samuel
Sang
Oaty
Nebo

20. Early Churches

Philippi, Antioch, Ephesus, Rome, and Corinth

21. Hidden Couplet About Paul

```
M A N I F O L D
D E M A N D E D
M I S S P E N T
M I N I S T E R
P R I S O N E R
C A S T A W A Y
H E A V E N L Y
R E W A S H E D
F A I T H F U L
T O U C H I N G
B R O T H E R S
B L A S T I N G
```

Old and spent, in prison cast,
He was faithful to the last.

22. They Would Not

| 1(e) | 3(i) | 5(c) | 7(j) | 9(h) |
| 2(d) | 4(b) | 6(g) | 8(f) | 10(a) |

23. The Gracious Ones

1(j)	Philemon	6(g)	II Kings 5:3
2(e)	Acts 16:14-15	7(c)	Gen. 24:18-19
3(f)	Acts 9:27	8(d)	Gen. 23:10-11
4(a)	Exod. 2:16-17	9(h)	II Sam. 23:16
5(b)	Gen. 13:8-9	10(i)	Ruth 2:16

24. If

1. Job (Job 14:14)
2. Martha (John 11:21)
3. Esther (Esther 4:16)
4. Hannah (I Sam. 1:9-11)
5. Elijah (I Kings 18:21)
6. Barak (Judg. 4:8)
7. Paul (Rom. 8:31)
8. Jephthah (Judg. 11:30-31)
9. Reuben (Gen. 42:37)
10. Jonathan (I Sam. 20:22)

25. Bible Crossword Puzzle in Numbers

¹3	²9		³3	⁴0	⁵0
⁶6	6		⁷0	1	1	7
	⁸9	⁹1	0		¹⁰5	7
		¹¹1	0		¹²0	7
	¹³8	9		¹⁴4	0	
¹⁵4	9		¹⁶9	0		
¹⁷6	9	¹⁸4	9	8		

26. Read Down and Find

C	C A I N	A I N	A I	N
O	O B E D	B E D	B E	D
M	S H E M	S H E	H E	S
E	E D E N	D E N	D N	E
A	A B E L	B E L	B L	E

27. Crowded Line

Gad (Head of a tribe — son of Jacob)
Adam (The first man)
Amos (A prophet)
Moses (A great leader)
Esther (A queen who saved her people)
Herodias (Herod's sister-in-law — Matt. 14:3)
Asa (Third king of Judah)
Sarah (Wife of a great patriarch)
Ara (A son of Jether — I Chron. 7:38)
Rahab (She sheltered spies — Josh. 2:1)
Ahab (A wicked king of Israel — I Kings 16:30)

28. "And of the Prophets" . . . and Others

1. Elijah (I King 18)
2. Elisha (II Kings 5)
3. Nathan (II Sam. 12:7)
4. Daniel (Dan. 2:16-19)
5. Nehemiah (Neh. 2.)
6. Jehoiada (II Kings 11:4-12)
7. Hezekiah (II Kings 19)
8. Deborah (Judg. 4)
9. Job (Job 19:25)
10. Hannah (I Sam. 1:24)

29. They Changed

1. The jailer (Acts 16:23-33)
2. Paul (Acts 9)
3. Moses (Exod. 4:10; Exod. 15)
4. The woman of Samaria (John 4:7-29)
5. Mark (Acts 15:37-38; II Tim 4:11)
6. Peter (Matt. 26:67-75; Acts 4:19)
7. Thomas (John 20:25-28)
8. Nicodemus (John 3:1; John 19:39-40)
9. Joseph (Gen. 37:1-7; Gen. 50:21)
10. Judah (Gen. 37:26-27; Gen. 44:18-34)

30. Heavenly Space

1(b)	Josh. 10:12	7(a)	Amos 5:8
2(a)	Josh. 10:12	8(c)	Job 9:9
3(c)	Josh. 10:12	9(c)	Luke 2:11 (Bethlehem)
4(a)	Josh. 10:13	10(c)	Isa. 47:13
5(b)	Job 9:9	11(c)	I Cor. 15:40-41
6(c)	Job 9:9	12(c)	

31. "The Unknown God"

```
I N H E R I T
H I M S E L F
W E L F A R E
S L I V E R S
M I N D F U L
S H I M M E R
S W E E T E R
R E M O V E D
W E E P I N G
C A N D A C E
N O T H I N G
G O S P E L S
O U T S I D E
T H I S T L E
P L O V E R S
```

In Him we live, In Him we move,
We can not go outside His love

32. Both Rhyme and Reason

1. Saul	4. Mark	7. Lot	10. Dan
2. Ruth	5. Cain	8. Rahab	11. Nun
3. Esther	6. Aquila	9. Acts	12. Hannah

33. Read the Square Clockwise

1. Cush	3. Shem	5. Esau	7. Adam	9. Anna
2. Ahab	4. Amos	6. Obed	8. Omri	10. Rama

34. Choice Within a Choice

1(b) I Sam. 20:20	4(a) II Kings 19 ff.	7(c) Josh 10:12
2(c) Ruth 1:16, 4:17	5(c) Dan. 6:24	8(a) Acts 17:6
3(a) I Kings 17:4	6(a) Psalm 137	

35. "Frustrations" in the Bible

1. Moses (Deut. 34)
2. David (I Chron. 17)
3. Jonah (Jon. 4)
4. Jephthah (Judg. 11)
5. Mary and Martha (John 11)
6. Hagar (Gen. 21)
7. Naomi (Ruth 1)
8. Eli (I Sam. 8)
9. Jacob (Gen. 29)
10. Elijah (I Kings 19)
11. Caleb and Joshua (Num. 13:30)
12. Paul (Acts 27)

36. Archaeological Discoveries

1(c) Exod. 5:1	6(h) I Kings 18:21
2(g) Josh. 2	7(e) Jon. 3
3(d) I Kings 9:15-19	8(f) Esther 1:2
4(j) II Kings 20:20	9(b) I Kings 22:39
5(i) Gen. 11:31	10(a) Dan. 5

37. "Now the Day Is Over

1. Abram (Gen. 15:12-13)
2. Jacob (Gen. 28:11-12)
3. Cleopas (Luke 24:13-29)
4. Isaac (Gen. 24:63-64)
5. Elijah (I Kings 18:36)
6. All (Luke 4:40)
7. The disciples — all but Thomas (John 20:19, 24)
8. Five loaves and two fishes (Matt. 14:15-20)
9. Rahab (Josh. 2:5)
10. Lazarus (John 12:2)

38. Word Acrostics

And ye shall return every man unto his family. Lev. 25:10

Reading Down: RELATIONS

A. R A N
   11 33 2

B. E A R
   5 23 20

C. L I L Y
   36 30 9 21

D. A R M E D
   1 15 34 17 3

E. T H U S
   13 29 14 31

F. I F
   35 32

G. O N L Y
   28 26 10 37

H. N A H U M
   16 8 7 25 22

I. S E V E N T Y
   6 12 18 19 24 27 4

39. Square of Squares

```
A B E L      M O A B
H    E Z R A      O
A    V    R       A
B E R I    A H A Z
     S          B
     A          E
J U D E    B E L A
O    L     A      M
H    A N N A      O
N O A H    L O I S
```

40. On the Way

1(h)	Matt. 21:9	7(k)	Acts 8:26-38
2(d)	Acts 9	8(c)	Gen. 27:5-12
3(e)	Luke 10:30	9(f)	Luke 24:13
4(a)	Acts 27	10(g)	Gen. 19
5(b)	Judg. 14:5-6	11(l)	Gen. 44
6(j)		12(i)	Luke 8:22-26

41. Find the Proverb

A good name is rather to be chosen than great riches. Prov. 22:1

42. Featuring Food

1. Daniel and his three friends (Dan. 1:8-15)
2. Esau (Gen. 25:34)
3. Elisha (II Kings 4:8-10)
4. The children of Israel (Exod. 16:15-18)
5. Joseph (Exod. 42:25)
6. John the Baptist (Matt. 3:4)
7. Elijah (I Kings 17:16)
8. Lazarus (Luke 16:20-21)
9. Jesus (Matt. 14:17-20)
10. The prodigal son (Luke 15:23)
11. Belshazzar (Dan. 5:1-6)
12. Ahab (I Kings 21:2)

43. Bird, Beast, and Insect

1(f)	I Kings 17:4	6(b)	II Sam. 18:9
2(j)	Gen. 8:11	7(h) and (e)	Judg. 14:8-14
3(a)	Prov. 6:6	8(i)	Jon. 4:7
4(d)	Exod. 10:14	9(g)	Matt. 10:29
5(e)	Dan. 6:23	10(c)	Gen. 41:18

44. Triple Proportion

1. Moses is to bold (meek) (Judg. 16:6; Gal. 3:9; Num. 12:3)
2. Esther is to deaconess (queen) (Judg. 4:14; Esther. 5:2; Luke 2:36)
3. Lois is to Timothy (Eunice) (I Sam. 1:29; II Tim. 1:5; Gen. 35:18)
4. Hagar is to Ishmael (she was his mother) (Ruth 1:2, 4; Gen. 21:3; Gen. 16:15)
5. Cain is to shepherd (tiller of the soil) (Gen. 25:27; Acts 18:3; Gen. 4:2)
6. Deacons is to 14 (7) (Acts 6:5)
7. Joshua is to Kish (Nun) (Exod. 33:11; I Sam. 16:20; Ruth 4:13-17)
8. Nebo is to brook (mountain) (I Sam. 17:2; Gen. 13:10; Deut. 34:1)
9. Genesis is to law (beginning) (dictionary)
10. David is to Jonathan (friend) (Matt. 4:21; I Sam. 20:16; Matt. 4:18)
11. Rahab is to Corinth (Jericho) (John 11:1; Acts 16:14; Josh. 2:1)

45. Acrostic

Rachel	Levite	Miriam	Jethro	Coney's
Reuben	Martha	Naboth	Savior	Garden
Isaiah	Esther	Olives	Ninety	Naaman
Jordan	Jacob's	Elijah	Peter's	Lystra

46. How Many

1. 66
2. 2 (Ps. 117)
3. 12 (Gen. 35:22)
4. 300 (Judg. 7:7)
5. 7 (Josh. 6:15-16)
6. 10 (Exod. 7-12)
7. 3 (Gen. 6:10)
8. 969 (Gen. 5:27)
9. 40
10. 5
11. 14 (Gen. 29:20-30)
12. 3
13. 12
14. 2 (raven and dove)
15. 7 (Acts 6:5)
16. 3 (Matt. 23:34)
17. 4 (Rev. 6)
18. 7 (Rev. 1:4)

47. The Parables

1(d)	Matt. 20:16		9(g)	Luke 15:5
2(j)	Matt. 13:5		10(i)	Luke 15:29
3(h)	Matt. 18:26		11(b)	Luke 14:18
4(f)	Matt. 13:30		12(c)	Matt. 25:8
5(n)	Luke 12:19		13(p)	Matt. 25:29
6(a)	Luke 10:31		14(e)	Luke 18:12 .
7(l)	Luke 13:19		15(o)	Matt. 21:37
8(m)	John 10:16		16(k)	Luke 13:8

48. Who?

1. Job / Samson
2. Solomon / Methuselah
3. Enoch / Jonah
4. Moses
5. Cain
6. Ruth
7. Rehoboam / Hoshea
8. The Good Samaritan
9. Paul / Caleb, Joshua and others
10. Isaiah (Isa. 6:8)
11. Peter
12. Shadrach, Meshach, and Abednego
13. David
14. Jesus
15. Nicodemus
16. Zacchaeus
17. Jacob
18. Gideon

49. "Dare to Be a Daniel"

```
D R E A M E D
A Z A R I A H
R E F U S E D
E T E R N A L
T R E M B L E
O U T W A R D
B A B Y L O N
E N E M I E S
A B S T A I N
D E L I V E R
A B I L I T Y
N O T H I N G
I N H E R I T
E X A M P L E
L I B E R T Y
```

50. Quote — Misquote

MISQUOTES:
1. Elisha should be Elijah
2. Pharaoh should be Herod
3. Herod should be Pilate
4. Eagles should be ravens
7. Ahab should be Pharaoh
9. Matthew should be Peter
10. Joshua should be Gideon

51. Sally's Complaint

eye to eye (Isa. 52:8)
feet of clay (Dan. 2:43)
turning the world upside down (Acts 17:6)
there is no discharge in that war (Eccles. 8:8)
a little here, a little there (Isa. 28:10)
ravenous as a wolf (Gen. 49:27)

52. "Judge" for Yourself

1(h)	Judg. 16:30		6(e)	Judg. 10:3-4
2(d)	Judg. 3:9-11		7(j)	Judg. 3:16-22
3(a)	Josh. 6:20		8(g)	Judg. 5:1
4(i)	Exod. 18:13-15		9(f)	Judg. 11:30-35
5(c)	I Sam. 8:6		10(b)	Judg. 6:39-40

53. The Nameless Ones

1(h)	Luke 17:12-16	7(g)	Acts 6:27-39
2(c)	II Kings 5:2-14	8(c)	Gen. 24 (his name is not given in this instance)
3(f)	Acts 23:16		
4(i)	John 4:7-26	9(d)	Judg. 11:36
5(a)	Matt. 15:22-28	10(j)	II Kings 4:10
6(b)	John 6:9		

54. "Name" the Italics

1. Esau
2. Leah
3. Deborah
4. Absalom
5. Hosea
6. Eli
7. Timothy
8. Abraham
9. Gideon
10. Andrew
11. Aquila
12. Silas

55. Down the Alphabet

Adam, (Gen. 4:1)
Boaz, (Ruth 2:3)
Caleb, (Num. 13:2, 6)
Dorcas, (Acts 9:39)
Esther, (Esther 2:17)
Festus, (Acts 25:8)
Gideon, (Judg. 8:17)
Hannah, (I Sam. 1:24)
Isaac, (Gen. 21:3)
Joseph, (Gen. 35:24)
Kish, (I Sam. 9:3)
Lydia, (Acts 16:15)
Moses, (Exod. 2:5)
Noah, (Gen. 7:17)
Orpah, (Ruth 1:6-18)
Paul, (Acts 25:12)
Quartus, (Rom. 16:21)
Ruth, (Ruth 1:18)
Samson, (Judg. 14:6)
Thomas, (John 20:25)
Uriah, (II Sam. 11:17)
Vashti, (Esther 2:17)
Zacchaeus, (Luke 19:2)

56. This Is _____ Speaking

1. Silas (Saul, Isaac, Laban, Aaron, Solomon)
2. Moses (Mary or Martha, Onesimus, Silas, Esau, Stephen)
3. Peter (Paul, Eve, Terah, Eli, Ruth)
4. Lois (Leah, Obed, Isaac, Samuel)
5. James (Joseph, Absalom, Moses, Elkanah, Sarah)

The second would not have been possible, as four were New Testament characters.

57. They Were "Human"

1. Martha (Luke 10:40)
2. Naomi (Ruth 3)
3. Rebekah (Gen. 27)
4. Moses (Exod. 18:17-24)
5. Lot (Gen. 13:8-11)
6. Samuel (I Sam. 8:1-3)
7. Joseph (Gen. 37:2)
8. Eli (I Sam. 2:12)
9. David (I Sam. 17:26-28)
10. David (II Sam. 18:33)

58. What Were They Doing?

1. Rounding up the disciples to bring them to Jerusalem (Acts 9:1-2)
2. Fishing (Matt. 4:18-19)
3. Drawing water (Gen. 24:15-16)
4. Looking for his father's asses (I Sam. 9)
5. Tending sheep (I Sam. 16:11-13)
6. Leading the sheep of his father-in-law (Exod. 3:1-2)
7. Fleeing from Esau (Gen. 27:42)
8. Ploughing (I Kings 19:19)
9. Collecting taxes (Matt. 9:9)
10. Serving a prison term (Gen. 41:14)
11. Threshing wheat (Judg. 6:11)

59. Questions in the Bible (Part 1)

1(j)	John 21:17	6(l)	Matt. 2:2	11(c)	Gen. 37:10
2(m)	Gen. 4:9	7(b)	Luke 10:40	12(g)	Esther 4:14
3(h)	John 14:5	8(a)	Jer. 8:22	13(d)	Acts 8:30
4(n)	Gen. 45:3	9(k)	I Cor. 15:55	14(f)	Gen. 22:7
5(o)	Job 14:14	10(e)	Ps. 8:3	15(i)	Matt. 22:17

60. Questions in the Bible (Part 2)

1(p)	John 18:38	6(c)	Mark 10:17	11(a)	Amos 3:3
2(n)	John 1:46	7(k)	Dan. 6:20	12(d)	Luke 21:7
3(m)	II Sam. 18:29	8(j)	Luke 10:29	13(e)	Isa. 53:1
4(l)	John 3:4	9(f)	Exod. 3:11	14(i)	Dan. 4:30
5(h)	John 12:5	10(b)	Rom. 8:31	15(g)	I Sam. 15:14